D1560578

U.S. COAST GUARD

FIGHTING FORCES

JASON COOPER

Rourke
Publishing LLC
Vero Beach, Florida 32964

www.rourkepublishing.com

PHOTO CREDITS: All photos courtesy of U.S. Coast Guard except pp 9, 17 courtesy of National Archives.

Title page: *The fire team of Coast Guard cutter* Chandeleur *hoses down a fire aboard a fishing boat off the coast of Florida. Firefighting at sea is one of many USCG duties.*

Editor: Frank Sloan

Cover and page design by Nicola Stratford

Library of Congress Cataloging-in-Publication Data

Cooper, Jason, 1942-
  U.S. Coast Guard / Jason Cooper.
     p. cm. — (Fighting forces)
Includes bibliographical references and index.
  ISBN 1-58952-714-3 (hardcover)
  1. United States. Coast Guard—Juvenile literature. [1. United States.
Coast Guard.] I. Title. II. Series: Cooper, Jason, 1942-   .
Fighting forces.
  VG53.C66 2003
  363.28'6'0973--dc21
                                                         2003005282

Printed in the USA

CG/CG

TABLE OF CONTENTS

THE COAST GUARD'S MANY JOBS

The U.S. Coast Guard is one of America's five **military**, or armed, services. Like the Army, Air Force, Navy, and Marines, the Coast Guard is prepared to fight. But fighting is not the Coast Guard's main duty. The Coast Guard has a big job in peacetime. In fact, the Coast Guard has many peacetime jobs! The Coast Guard serves along the nation's seashores and big inland waters. Its duties start with almost anything that has to do with boats and boating.

The Coast Guard cutter Washington, *on patrol,* ▶ *cruises past Honolulu's Waikiki beach.*

The Coast Guard began more than 200 years ago. Its job then was to protect America's shorelines from pirates and **smugglers**. Later, the Coast Guard began rescuing ships and sailors. The Coast Guard has far more jobs now than it did then. But it continues to be America's ocean police and rescue squad, among other things.

▲ *Members of a Coast Guard crew rescue a survivor from a fishing boat accident near the Hawaiian Island of Kauai.*

The Coast Guard has fought in America's biggest wars. It has rescued thousands of people at sea. And by enforcing laws of the sea, it has saved many people from disaster.

The Coast Guard's on-duty force is made up of about 35,000 men and women. More than 8,000 people are in the Coast Guard **Reserve**. About 34,000 more serve in the Coast Guard **Auxiliary**. Some 5,000 **civilians** work for the Coast Guard.

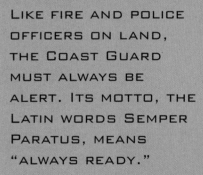

FACT FILE ★

LIKE FIRE AND POLICE OFFICERS ON LAND, THE COAST GUARD MUST ALWAYS BE ALERT. ITS MOTTO, THE LATIN WORDS SEMPER PARATUS, MEANS "ALWAYS READY."

THE COAST GUARD AT WORK

CHAPTER TWO

One of the Coast Guard's big jobs is the defense of the nation, or "national defense." In wartime, the Coast Guard becomes part of the U.S. Navy. Coast guard **vessels** guard larger Navy ships. Coast Guard ships guard shipping lanes. They use their guns to fire on enemy ships and planes. They are especially alert for enemy submarines.

In March, 2003, Coast Guard vessels were sent to the Persian Gulf to help in war against Iraq, known as Operation Iraqi Freedom.

FACT FILE ★

IN PEACETIME, THE COAST GUARD HELPS DEFEND THE NATION BY WATCHING FOR **TERRORIST** ACTIVITY. THIS IS ONE PART OF THE COAST GUARD'S EFFORTS AT CREATING A SAFE, SECURE HOMELAND.

▲ *U.S. troops go over the side of a combat transport ship manned by the Coast Guard. The troops began the invasion of Bougainville in November, 1943, during World War II.*

For its **maritime** safety mission, the Coast Guard has nearly 200 **law enforcement** and search and rescue stations. These stations are located along American shores. The Coast Guard has ships, boats, and aircraft always ready for rescue work.

The Coast Guard's education program helps boaters and ship captains learn how to be safe at sea. For example, the Coast Guard teaches several classes about proper boat safety and operation. And the Coast Guard decides which safety equipment, such as life jackets, is made properly.

The Coast Guard also reports dangerous weather conditions to the U.S. Weather Service. The Coast Guard's International Ice Patrol finds and follows icebergs in the North Atlantic Ocean.

◀ *An HH-65 Dolphin helicopter from the Coast Guard Air Station at Traverse City, Michigan, begins a search and rescue flight. The Coast Guard is active on the Great Lakes.*

When accidents happen at sea, the Coast Guard's search and rescue job begins. Finding a boat in trouble can be a huge job. America has more than 95,000 miles (152,000 kilometers) of coastline. And Coast Guard ships and aircraft often have to rescue sailors far from shore.

Another Coast Guard mission is to make sure that waterways remain useful to boats and ships. That means marking open channels so that vessels do not hit undersea objects. The Coast Guard sets up lights, foghorns, beacons, and markers called **buoys**. Special Coast Guard ships called icebreakers keep frozen channels open.

The Coast Guard's C-130 Hercules planes are often used on long distance search and rescue operations. ▶

Like the early Coast Guard, the modern Coast Guard fights the smuggling of drugs and other **illegal** goods. It also tries to prevent the arrival of illegal **aliens**. Aliens are people who live in the United States without U.S. citizenship.

The Coast Guard helps protect the natural resources of the sea, too. Many laws protect sea life and the quality of seawater itself. But not every ship or shipping company obeys the laws. The Coast Guard, for example, checks the catches of fishing boats. A captain whose boat breaks fishing laws can be fined. The boat can even be taken.

▲ *A Coast Guard icebreaker smashes its way through the ice of Antarctica. Coast Guard ships assist American researchers here on the planet's coldest continent.*

Polluters are another problem. Ships may drop garbage, oil, or chemicals into the sea, causing pollution. Reports of polluters bring the Coast Guard quickly. The Coast Guard directed a major cleanup of oil along the Alaska coast in 1989. That spill was the result of a tanker, the *Exxon Valdez*, going aground.

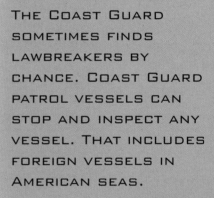

FACT FILE ★

THE COAST GUARD SOMETIMES FINDS LAWBREAKERS BY CHANCE. COAST GUARD PATROL VESSELS CAN STOP AND INSPECT ANY VESSEL. THAT INCLUDES FOREIGN VESSELS IN AMERICAN SEAS.

THE COAST GUARD COMMAND

Each of America's armed services is under the control of an organization called a department. Each department is part of the U.S. Government. All of America's armed services are under the U.S. Department of Defense—except the Coast Guard.

The Coast Guard has been part of the U.S. Department of Transportation for many years. But it's not quite that simple. If war is declared by the United States, the Coast Guard becomes part of the Navy. And the Navy is part of the Department of Defense. During World War II (1939-1945), for instance, the Coast Guard was under that department. The president of the United States can also act to make the Coast Guard part of the Navy at any time.

HIGHEST RANKS
IN DESCENDING ORDER
ADMIRAL
VICE ADMIRAL
REAR ADMIRAL
CAPTAIN
COMMANDER
LIEUTENANT COMMANDER
LIEUTENANT
LIEUTENANT JUNIOR GRADE
ENSIGN

▲ *Marines hold up a sign to thank their Coast Guard brothers after battling the Japanese for the island of Guam in August, 1944.*

In late 2002, the U.S. Government created the new Department of Homeland Security. The new department brought many organizations from other departments together. One of the organizations to join this department is the U.S. Coast Guard.

Departments are headed up by civilians. Like the other armed services, then, the Coast Guard is under civilian leadership.

▲ Recruits receive orders before boarding the Coast Guard training ship Eagle at the U. S. Naval Station in Puerto Rico.

LIFE IN THE COAST GUARD

Young people who wish to join the U.S. Coast Guard must be at least 17 years old. They can be no older than 27.

These Coast Guard recruits attend eight weeks of basic training at the Coast Guard center in Cape May, New Jersey. Coast Guard sailors learn about many skills they will need in the service. Some of the skills are firefighting, communications, first aid, and seamanship. Seamanship teaches recruits basic facts about operating a boat. It also teaches how to tell direction at sea. Recruits learn about Coast Guard weapons and military marching, discipline, and parade.

FACT FILE ★

OTHER COAST GUARD RECRUITS BECOME OFFICERS BY ATTENDING OFFICER CANDIDATE SCHOOL. OCS IS A 17-WEEK PROGRAM FOR YOUNG MEN AND WOMEN WITH COLLEGE DEGREES. OCS IS HELD AT THE COAST GUARD ACADEMY.

Military services have members of several different ranks. Higher ranking members are called officers. The Coast Guard trains many of its officers at the U.S. Coast Guard Academy on the Thames River in New London, Connecticut. The Coast Guard Academy is a college. Students graduate as officers in the Coast Guard, but they also earn a college degree.

▲ Cadets march in front of Hamilton Hall at the U.S. Coast Guard Academy, New London, Connecticut.

WEAPONS AND EQUIPMENT

CHAPTER FIVE

The Coast Guard has nearly 100 ships and many more boats, which are smaller vessels. Some of the vessels are icebreakers, patrol boats, buoy tenders, tugboats, and cutters.

"Cutter" is a term with roots in early Coast Guard history. The 18th century Coast Guard cutters were wooden ships with cloth sails. Today the term "cutter" applies to almost any Coast Guard vessel more than 65 feet (20 meters) in length. The Coast Guard considers any cutter more than 180 feet (55 m) long to be a "large" cutter. The Coast Guard has cutters, however, in the 400-foot (122-m) range.

Coast Guard sailors and their vessels have a variety of weapons. They vary from pistols and M-16 rifles to cannons. The larger cutters have the greatest firepower. The Navy often trains crews of the large cutters.

▲ *The Coast Guard cutter* Spencer *passes by the Statue of Liberty in New York harbor. Coast guard cutters keep a watchful eye for smugglers and terrorists.*

THE COAST GUARD'S EARLY DAYS

Shortly after the United States was formed, Congress acted to create the Coast Guard. In 1790 the Coast Guard was called the Revenue Marine. It had perhaps 10 ships, and its job was to police American ports. Stop the smugglers, Congress said, and make sure taxes—**revenues**—are paid by shippers.

The new service's job and boundaries grew quickly. The Revenue Marine became the Revenue Cutter Service. It fought French vessels in 1798-1800. It fought British ships in the War of 1812 (1812-1815).

The modern Coast Guard, shown here on patrol in San Francisco Bay, brought together many government organizations. ▶

In 1822 the cutter *Louisiana* helped U.S. and British navy ships capture five pirate vessels in the Caribbean Sea. The Coast Guard was active with the Navy during the Civil War (1861-1865) to block ships from reaching Southern port cities.

Meanwhile, other government departments were busy with other kinds of maritime work. There were people operating lighthouses and people inspecting steamboats. They were people making sure that waterways could be used easily. In the mid-1800s the government built lifesaving stations along U.S. coasts. And in 1871 it created the Lifesaving Service. Eventually, the lifesaving, lighthouse, and several other organizations were joined with the Revenue Cutter Service as the U.S. Coast Guard.

The Coast Guard is always ready to help, even in the worst weather! Crew members of the cutter Evergreen *use baseball bats to remove ice while on a winter fisheries patrol.* ▶

During World War I (1914-1918) Coast Guard vessels guarded naval warships in Europe. Some of its ships guarded Navy vessels. Others looked for enemy submarines and patrolled the American coasts.

In World War II the Coast Guard was again under Navy control. Ships manned by Coast Guard sailors sank 11 submarines. Coast guard patrols walked beaches and drove along coastal highways. At sea, the Coast Guard rescued more than 1,500 people from sinking ships near the U.S. coast.

In the 21st century the U.S. Coast Guard is rapidly improving its lineup of aircraft and vessels. New equipment is replacing old. The Coast Guard will always be ready. "Semper paratus."

◀ *The Coast Guard practices drills in rough seas in order to be prepared to assist anyone in distress during bad weather.*

GLOSSARY

aliens (AYE lee uhnz) — people who live in the United States, but without U.S. citizenship

auxiliary (ox ILL yah ree) — offering or providing help

buoys (BOO eez) — floating markers tied to the bottom of a waterway

civilians (SUH vil yuns) — people who are not members of the armed forces

illegal (ill EE guhl) — against the law

law enforcement (LAWH EN forse munt) — the efforts and organizations that serve to uphold laws; police work

maritime (MAH ruh time) — having to do with the sea

military (MIL uh tare ee) —having to do with or being part of the nation's armed forces

polluters (puh LOOT urz) — people who put harmful substances into the air, ground, or sea

recruits (ruh KROOTZ) — people who join a military service

reserve (REE SURV) — non-active soldiers who may be called to active duty in a national emergency

revenues (REV uh nyewz) — sums of money that are collected

smugglers (SMUG glurz) — people who sneak illegal goods into a place

terrorist (TARE uhr ist) — one who uses terror, such as bombings of civilian targets, to further a cause

vessels (VESS uhlz) — boats or ships

INDEX

FURTHER READING

Gaines, Ann Graham. *The Coast Guard in Action*.
    Enslow, 2001
Weintraub, Aileen. *Life Inside the Coast Guard
    Academy.* Children's Press, 2002.

WEBSITE TO VISIT

www.uscg.mil

ABOUT THE AUTHOR

Jason Cooper has written several children's books
about a variety of topics for Rourke Publishing, including
the recent series *Eye to Eye with Big Cats.*